2

20

16

Wrap your precious baby in these adorable blankets to crochet!

5

8

18

12

LEISURE ARTS, INC. • Maumelle, Arkansas

Sweet Ribbons Blanket

INTERMEDIATE

SHOPPING LIST

Yarn (Worsted Weight) MEDIUM 4
[3.5 ounces, 180 yards
(100 grams, 165 meters) per ball]:

- ☐ Main Color - White 6 balls

(Worsted Weight)
[2.8 ounces, 160 yards
(80 grams, 146 meters) per ball]:

- ☐ Color C- Variegated 2 balls

(Worsted Weight)
[3.5 ounces, 200 yards
(100 grams, 182 meters) per ball]:

- ☐ Color A- Pink 70 yds.
- ☐ Color B- Blue 70 yds.
- ☐ Color D- Yellow 70 yds.
- ☐ Color E- Green 70 yds.

Crochet Hook

- ☐ Size H-8 (5.00 mm) or size needed for gauge

SIZE INFORMATION

Size: 33" x 39" [84 cm x 99 cm]

GAUGE INFORMATION

8 dc plus ch-3 to 3" [7.5 cm] and 6 rows to 3.25" [8 cm] measured over pattern, using **suggested** hook or any size hook which will give the correct stitch gauge.

Please Note: Ribbons will be woven through the ch-3 sps.

INSTRUCTIONS

To Make Blanket: Using MC, ch 101.

Row 1: Dc in 4th ch from hook (3 skipped ch count as 1st dc), dc in each of next 6 ch, *ch 3, skip next 3 ch, dc in each of next 7 ch; rep from * to last ch, dc in last ch - 72 dc and 9 ch-3 sps.

Row 2: Ch 3 (counts as 1st dc now and throughout), turn, dc in each of next 7 dc, *ch 3, skip next ch-3 sp, dc in each of next 7 dc; rep from * to last dc, dc in last dc - 72 dc and 9 ch-3 sps.

Rows 3-9: Work as Row 2.

Row 10: Ch 3, turn, dc in each of next 2 dc, *ch 3, skip next 3 dc, dc in each of next 2 dc, ch 3, skip next ch-3 sp, dc in each of next 2 dc; repeat from * to last 6 dc, ch 3, skip next 3 dc, dc in each of last 3 dc - 42 dc and 19 ch-3 sps.

Row 11: Ch 3, turn, dc in each of next 2 dc, 3 dc in next ch-3 sp, dc in each of next 2 dc, *ch 3, dc in each of next 2 dc, 3 dc in next ch-3 sp, dc in each of next 2 dc; repeat from * to last dc, dc in last dc - 72 dc and 9 ch-3 sps.

Rows 12-47: Repeat Rows 3 through 11 four times more.

Rows 48-54: Work as Row 2.

DO NOT FASTEN OFF, ruffle will be worked once the ribbons have been made and woven into place.

To Make Horizontal Ribbons: (make one in each contrast color)

Ch 101 loosely, dc in 4th ch from hook and in each ch across - 99 dc. Fasten off.

Using color picture as guide, weave ribbons into blanket through the ch-3 sps.

Starting at bottom of blanket, work ribbons in the following color sequence: Color B, Color A, Color C, Color E, then Color D.

Once the ribbons have been woven in, pin each end of ribbon in place to hold them until ruffle is worked.

To Make Vertical Ribbons:

Make two ribbons each of Colors A, B, D and E, then one ribbon of Color C (center ribbon),

Ch 102 loosely, dc in 4th ch from hook and in each ch across - 100 dc. Fasten off.

Weave the vertical ribbons, starting at right side of blanket and working across in the following color sequence: Color B, Color A, Color E, Color D, Color C (center ribbon), Color D, Color E, Color A, thenColor B.

Again, once the ribbons have been woven in, pin each end of ribbon in place to hold them until ruffle is worked.

Ruffle Edging: With right side of blanket facing, and using MC (still attached), work as follows:

Rnd 1: Ch 1, do NOT turn, work 3 sc in end of each row along both sides of blanket (being sure to work over ends of each ribbon as you come to it), 3 sc in each corner, then sc in each ch stitch across bottom edge of blanket, and sc in each dc across top edge (being sure to work over ends of each ribbon as you come to them), join with sl st in first sc.

Rnd 2: Ch 3, dc in same st, 2 dc in each sc around entire outside edge of blanket, join with sl st in top of beg ch-3. Fasten off.

Rnd 3: Join Color C in any dc, ch 3, dc in each dc around, join with sl st in top of beg ch-3. Fasten off.

Rnd 4: Join MC in any dc, ch 3, dc in each dc around, join with sl st in top of beg ch-3. Fasten off.

Close up view of working over the end of a Ribbon

Scalloped Border Blanket

INTERMEDIATE

SHOPPING LIST

Yarn (Dk/Sport Weight) FINE 2

[1.75 ounces, 171 yards (50 grams, 156 meters) per ball]:

- ☐ Lavender 10 balls

Crochet Hook

- ☐ Size 7 (4.5 mm) or size needed for gauge

SIZE INFORMATION

Size: 32" x 40" [81 cm x 101.5 cm]

GAUGE INFORMATION

16 sts to 4" [10 cm] and 10 rows to 3" [7.5 cm] measured over pattern, using **suggested** hook or any size hook which will give the correct stitch gauge.

STITCH GUIDE

Shell - (2 tr, ch 2, 2 tr) in sp indicated.

V-st - (tr, ch 2, tr) in sp indicated.

Picot - Ch 3, sl st in first ch.

INSTRUCTIONS

To Make: Ch 109.

Row 1: Sc in 2nd ch from hook and in each ch to end - 108 sc.

Row 2: Ch 1, turn, sc in first st, dc in next st, *sc in next st, dc in next st; rep from * to end.

Repeat Row 2 for pattern until piece measures about 35" [89 cm] from beg.

Next Row: Ch 1, turn, sc in each st across.

Border:

Rnd 1: Ch 4 (counts as first hdc, ch 2), turn, *skip next 2 sts, hdc in next st, (ch 2, skip next st, hdc in next st) across to last 2 sts (adjusting skipped sts if necessary), ch 2, skip next st, (hdc, ch 2, hdc) in last st for corner - (53 ch-2 loops, not including corners); now working into ends of rows along side edge, (ch 2, skip next row, hdc in next row) across to last last row, ch 2, skip last row (adjusting sts if necessary)**, (hdc, ch 2, hdc) in next corner, ch 2 - (105 ch-2 loops not including corners); rep from * to ** once more, hdc in same st as beg ch-4, ch 1, sc in 2nd ch of beg ch-4 to form last ch-2 sp.

Rnd 2: Ch 5 (counts as tr, ch 2), tr in same corner - Beg V-st made, *(ch 2, Shell in next loop, ch 2, skip next 2 loops, V-st in next loop, skip next 2 loops) across to last 2 loops before next corner sp, ending last rep at V-st in next loop, ch 2, skip next loop, Shell in last loop, V-st in corner ch-2 loop, now working along side edge,ch 2, skip next loop, Shell in next loop,(ch 2, skip next 2 loops, V-st in next loop, ch 2, skip next 2 loops, Shell in next loop) across to last loop before next corner loop, ch 2, skip last loop*, V-st in corner ch-2 loop; rep from * to * once more, join with sl st in 3rd ch of beg ch-5.

Rnd 3: Sl st into corner ch-2, (ch 4, 9 tr) in same sp, ch 2, 2 hdc in ch-sp of next Shell, *ch 2, 10 tr in next V-st, ch 2, 2 hdc in ch-sp of next Shell; rep from * around, ch 2, join with sl st in top of beg ch-4.

Rnd 4: Ch 5 (counts as tr and ch 1), [tr next tr, ch 1] 9 times, hdc in sp between next two hdc, *ch 1, [tr in next tr, ch 1] 10 times, hdc in sp between next 2 hdc; rep from * around, ch 1, join with sl st in 4th ch of beg ch-5.

Rnd 5: *[Sl st in next ch-1 sp, Picot] 9 times, sl st in each of next two ch-1 sps; rep from * around, join with sl st in first sl st. Fasten off. Weave in all ends.

Close up view of scallop edge

Butterfly Afghan

INTERMEDIATE

SHOPPING LIST

Yarn (Dk/Sport Weight) FINE 2

[1.75 ounces, 171 yards (50 grams, 156 meters) per ball]:

- ☐ Lavender 7 balls

Crochet Hook

- ☐ Size F-5 (3.75 mm) or size needed for gauge

SIZE INFORMATION

Size: 37" x 37" [94 cm x 94 cm]

GAUGE INFORMATION

9 dc and 4 rows to 2" [5 cm] measured over double crochet using **suggested** hook or any size hook which will give the correct stitch gauge.

Note: Ch 3 at the beg of each row counts as beg dc. When working the pattern, both dc and ch sts (each ch counts as one st), are referred to as "sts" for counting the following row.

INSTRUCTIONS

To Make: Ch 156.

Row 1: Dc in 4th ch from hook (skipped ch sts count as dc) and in each ch across - 154 dc.

Row 2: Ch 3, turn, dc in each of the next 3 dc,*[ch 2, skip next 2 dc, dc in next dc] 15 times, dc in each of next 6 dc; rep from * twice, but ending last rep with dc in each of last 3 dc.

Row 3: Ch 3, turn, dc in each of next 3 dc, *[ch 2, skip next 2 sts, dc in next dc] 6 times, dc in each of the next 2 ch, dc in next dc, ch 2, dc in next dc, dc in each of next 2 ch, dc in next dc, [ch 2, skip next 2 sts, dc in next dc] 6 times, dc in each of next 6 dc; rep from * twice, but ending last rep with dc in each of last 3 dc.

Row 4: Ch 3, turn, dc in each of next 3 dc,*[ch 2, skip next 2 sts, dc in next dc] 6 times, ch 2, skip next 2 sts, dc in next dc, dc in each of next 3 sts (both ch-sp and dc), [ch 2, skip next 2 sts, dc in next dc] 7 times, dc in each of next 6 dc; rep from * twice, but ending last rep with dc in each of last 3 dc.

Row 5: Ch 3, turn, dc in each of next 3 dc, *[ch 2, skip next 2 sts, dc in next dc] 3 times, dc in each of next 3 sts, [ch 2, skip next 2 sts (either ch or dc) dc in next dc] 7 times, dc in each of next 3 sts, [ch 2, skip next 2 sts, dc in next dc] 3 times, dc in each of next 6 dc; rep from * twice, but ending last rep with dc in each of last 3 dc.

Row 6: Ch 3, turn, dc in each of next 3 dc, *[ch 2, skip next 2 sts, dc in next dc] twice, dc in each of next 9 sts, [ch 2, skip next 2 sts, dc in next dc] 5 times, dc in each of next 9 sts, [ch 2, skip next 2 sts, dc in next dc] twice, dc in each of next 6 dc; rep from * twice, but ending last rep with dc in each of last 3 dc.

Row 7: Ch 3, turn, dc in each of next 3 dc, *[ch 2, skip next 2 sts, dc in next dc] twice, dc in each of next 3 dc, ch 2, skip next 2 dc, dc in each of next 4 dc, [ch 2, skip next 2 sts, dc in next dc] twice, dc in each of next 3 sts, [ch 2, skip next 2 sts, dc in next dc] twice, dc in each of next 3 dc, ch 2, skip next 2 dc, dc in each of next 4 dc, [ch 2, skip next 2 sts, dc in next dc] twice, dc in each of next 6 dc; rep from * twice, but ending last rep with dc in each of last 3 dc.

Row 8: Ch 3, turn, dc in each of next 3 dc, *[ch 2, skip next 2 sts, dc in next dc] twice, dc in each of next 12 sts, ch 2, dc in each of next 4 dc, ch 2, skip next 2 sts, dc in each of next 13 sts, [ch 2, skip next 2 sts, dc in next dc] twice, dc in each of next 6 dc; rep from * twice, but ending last rep with dc in each of last 3 dc.

Row 9: Ch 3, turn, dc in each of next 3 dc, *[ch 2, skip next 2 sts, dc in next dc] twice, dc in each of next 12 sts, ch 2, dc in next 4 dc, ch 2, skip next 2 sts, dc in each of next 13 sts, [ch 2, skip next 2 sts, dc in next dc] twice, dc in each of next 6 dc; rep from * twice, but ending last rep with dc in each of last 3 dc.

Row 10: Ch 3, turn, dc in each of next 3 dc, *[ch 2, skip next 2 sts, dc in next dc] 6 times, dc in each of next 9 sts, [ch 2, skip next 2 sts, dc in next dc] 6 times, dc in each of next 6 dc; rep from * twice, but ending last rep with dc in each of last 3 dc.

Row 11: Ch 3, turn, dc in each of next 3 dc, *[ch 2, skip next 2 sts, dc in next dc] 3 times, dc in each of the next 27 sts, [ch 2, skip next 2 sts, dc in next dc] 3 times, dc in each of next 6 dc; rep from * twice, but ending last rep with dc in each of last 3 dc.

Row 12: Ch 3, turn, dc in each of next 3 dc, *[ch 2, skip next 2 sts, dc in next dc] twice, dc in each of next 33 sts, [ch 2, skip next 2 sts, dc in next dc] twice, dc in each of next 6 dc; rep from * twice, but ending last rep with dc in each of last 3 dc.

Row 13: Ch 3, turn, dc in each of next 3 dc, *ch 2, dc in next dc, dc in each of next 39 sts, ch 2, dc in next dc, dc in each of next 6 dc; rep from * twice, but ending last rep with dc in each of last 3 dc.

Row 14: Ch 3, turn, dc in each of next 3 dc, *ch 2, dc in next dc, dc in each of next 6 dc, ch 2, skip next 2 dc, dc in each of next 7 dc, ch 2, skip next 2 dc, dc in each of next 4 dc, ch 2, skip next 2 dc, dc in each of next 7 dc, ch 2, skip next 2 dc, dc in each of next 7 dc, ch 2, dc in next dc, dc in each of next 6 dc; rep from * twice, but ending last rep with dc in each of last 3 dc.

Row 15: Ch 3, turn, dc in each of next 3 dc, *ch 2, dc in next dc, dc in each of next 12 sts, ch 2, skip next 2 dc, dc in next dc, ch 2, dc in each of next 4 dc, ch 2, dc in next dc, ch 2, skip next 2 dc, dc in each of next 13 sts, ch 2, dc in next dc, dc in each of next 6 dc; rep from * twice, but ending last rep with dc in each of last 3 dc.

Row 16: Ch 3, turn, dc in each of next 3 dc, *ch 2, dc in each of next 10 dc, ch 2, skip next 2 dc, dc in next dc, ch 2, dc in each of next 4 sts, ch 2, skip next 2 dc, dc in each of next 4 sts, ch 2, dc in next dc, ch 2, skip next 2 dc, dc in each of next 10 dc, ch 2, dc in next dc, dc in each of next 6 dc; rep from * twice, but ending last rep with dc in each of last 3 dc.

Row 17: Ch 3, turn, dc in each of next 3 dc, *[ch 2, skip next 2 sts, dc in next st] 5 times, dc in each of next 3 sts, [ch 2, skip next 2 sts, dc in next st] 3 times, dc in each of next 3 sts, [ch 2, skip next 2 sts, dc in next st] 5 times, dc in each of next 6 dc; rep from * twice, but ending last rep with dc in each of last 3 dc.

Row 18: Ch 3, turn, dc in each of next 3 dc, *[ch 2, skip next 2 sts, dc in next dc] 4 times, dc in each of next 3 sts, [ch 2, skip next 2 sts, dc in next st] 5 times, dc in each of next 3 sts, [ch 2, skip next 2 sts, dc in next dc] 4 times, dc in each of next 6 dc; rep from * twice, but ending last rep with dc in each of last 3 dc.

Row 19: Ch 3, turn, dc in each of next 3 dc, *[ch 2, skip next 2 sts, dc in next st] 7 times, dc in each of next 3 sts, [ch 2, skip next 2 sts, dc in next st] 7 times, dc in each of next 6 dc; rep from * twice, but ending last rep with dc in each of last 3 dc.

Rows 20-70: Repeat Rows 3-19 three times more.

Row 71: Repeat Row 2. Do not fasten off.

Edging: Ch 1, turn, work 2 sc in first st, *sc in each st across to corner, work 3 sc in corner; now working along side of afghan; work 2 sc in each row across to next corner, work 3 sc in next corner; rep from * once more, ending with sc in first corner, join with slip st to first sc. Fasten off.

Weave in all ends.

Design by Bernette Sharp.

Choo Choo Blankie

INTERMEDIATE

SHOPPING LIST

Yarn (Fingering Weight) SUPER FINE 1

[1.75 ounces, 230 yards (50 grams, 210 meters) per ball]:

- ☐ Blue 7 balls

Crochet Hook

- ☐ Size E-4 (3.50 mm) or size needed for gauge

SIZE INFORMATION

Size: 29" x 40" [73.5 cm x 102 cm]

GAUGE INFORMATION

22 sts and 12 rows to 4" [10 cm] measured over pattern using **suggested** hook or any size hook which will give the correct stitch gauge.

Note: Blankie is worked from a Graph, with each square representing either a filled square (dc in each of next 2 sts) or an open square (ch 1, skip next dc or ch-sp, dc in next dc or ch-sp).

Each row begins with ch 4 (counts as dc, ch 1), skip first ch-sp which is **NOT** shown on the graph.

Each row ends with ch 1, dc in 3rd ch of turning ch, also **NOT** shown on the graph.

Both are given in the written directions for the first few rows, continue to work the beg and end throughout.

Each ch-sp on the Graph is counted as a stitch.

INSTRUCTIONS

To Make: Ch 169.

Now proceed to work Graph as follows:

Row 1: (right side) Dc in 5th ch from hook (4 skipped sts count as dc, ch 1), *ch 1, skip next ch, dc in next ch; rep from * to end - 167 sts (including ch-1 sps) or 81 squares on the graph, not including the beg and end of each row.

Row 2: Ch 4 (counts as dc, ch 1 throughout), turn,skip first ch-sp, dc in next dc, now dc in each dc and ch-sp across to last ch- sp, ch 1, dc in 3rd ch of turning ch - 167 sts.

Row 3: Ch 4, turn, skip first ch-sp, dc in next dc,dc in each of next 2 dc (first block on graph), *ch 1, skip next dc, dc in next dc; rep from * to last 4 sts, dc in each of next 2 dc (last block on graph), ch 1, dc in 3rd ch of turning ch.

Rows 4 and 5: Ch 4, turn, skip first ch-sp, dc in next dc,dc in each of next 2 dc (first block), *ch 1, skip next ch-sp, dc in next dc; rep from * to last 4 sts, dc in each of next 2 dc (last block), ch 1, dc in 3rd ch of turning ch.

Row 6: Ch 4, turn, skip first ch-sp, dc in next dc, now dc in each dc and ch-sp across to last ch-sp, ch 1, dc in 3rd ch of turning ch.

Continue to follow Graph, beg and ending each row as set until 47 rows have been completed.

Repeat Rows 6 through 47 once more, then Rows 6 through 27 once.

Please Note: The last rep of the train was worked incorrectly on the model shown.

By working Rows 6-27 as instructed, the last train will run in the alternate direction as it should.

Now work Row 1 once more, do not fasten off.

Edging:

Rnd 1: Work [sc, ch 3] 3 times in corner, working across the side of blankie, around dc at ends of rows, *(sc, ch 3) evenly across to next corner (be sure to keep the sts spaced evenly so that the side edges don't ruffle), [sc, ch 3] 3 times in corner**, now working along bottom edge of blankie, (sc, ch 3) in each ch-sp across to next corner, [sc, ch 3] 3 times in corner, rep from * to ** across other side edge.

Now working in ch-1 sps of last row, (sc, ch 3) in each ch-1 sp across, join with sl st in first sc.

Rnd 2: Sl st to second ch-3 of corner, 7 dc in same sp, *ch 1, skip next ch-3 sp, sc in next ch-3 sp, ch 1, skip next ch-3 sp, 5 dc in next ch-3 sp; rep from * to next corner, adjusting as necessary to end with skip first ch-3 sp of corner, 7 dc in center ch-3 sp; rep from * around entire outside edge of blankie, join with sl st in first dc. Fasten off. Weave in all ends.

Design by Cindy Hane.

GRAPH

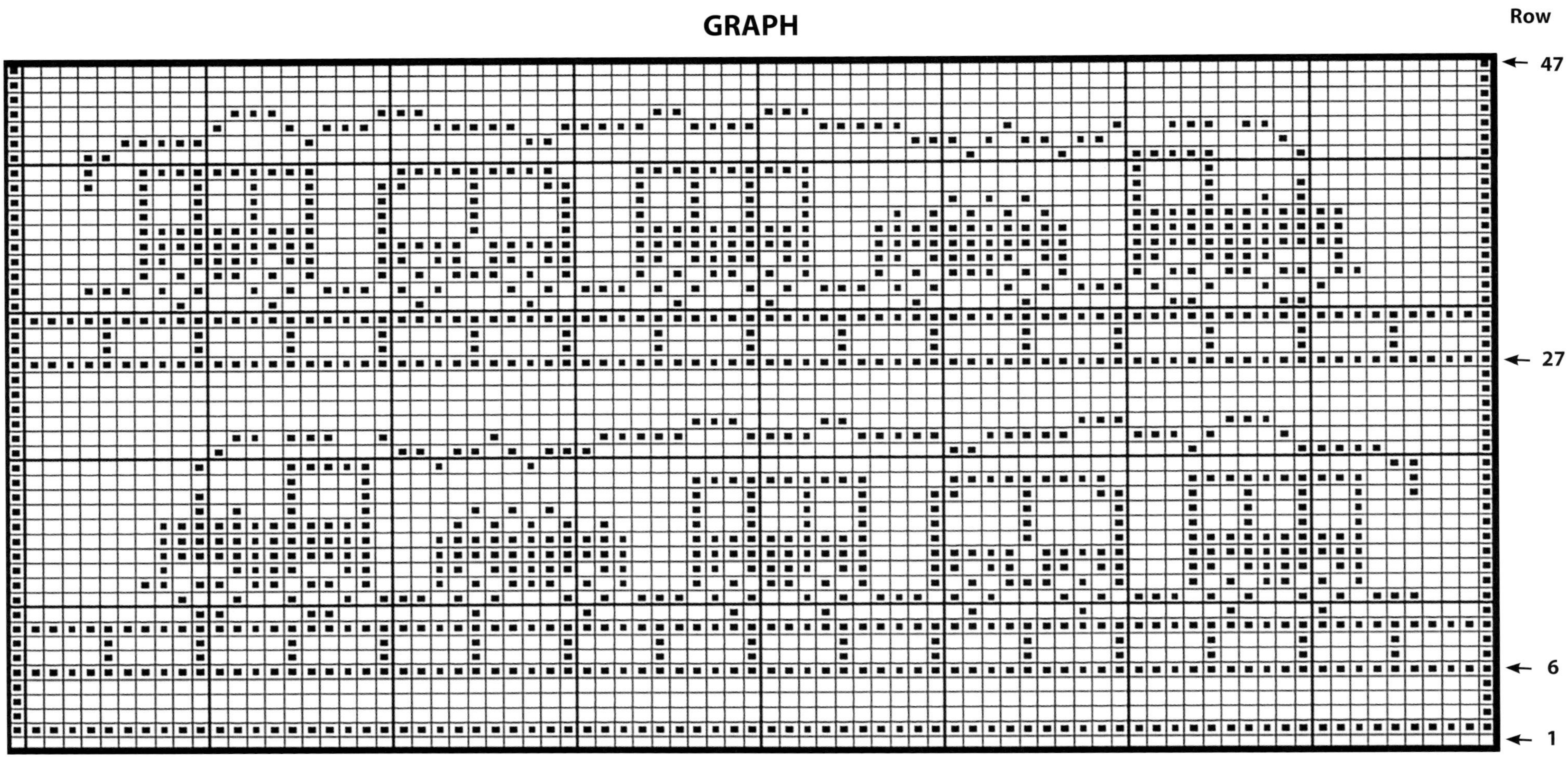

READ WRONG SIDE ROWS FROM THIS SIDE

READ RIGHT SIDE ROWS FROM THIS SIDE

STITCH GUIDE

☐ Ch 1, skip next st, dc in next st

■ Dc in each of next 2 sts.

Remember, Graph does NOT show
Ch 4, skip first ch-sp, dc in next dc at beg of each row
OR
ch 1, dc in 3rd ch of turning ch at end of each row.

Baby Swirls Blanket

INTERMEDIATE

SHOPPING LIST

Yarn (Dk/Sport Weight) FINE 2

[1.75 ounces, 171 yards

(50 grams, 156 meters) per ball]:

- ☐ Pink 3 balls
- ☐ Green 3 balls
- ☐ White 3 balls
- ☐ Blue 3 balls

Crochet Hook

- ☐ Size G-6 (4.00 mm)
  or size needed for gauge

SIZE INFORMATION

Size: 38" x 40.5" [96.5 cm x 103 cm]

GAUGE INFORMATION

Each panel should measure 4.25" [10.5 cm] wide and the Base and First Swirl should measure 3.25" [8 cm] long, using **suggested** hook or any size hook which will give the correct stitch gauge.

INSTRUCTIONS

To Make: Make 8 panels in total, working 2 panels in each color.

Base: Ch 6, join with sl st in first ch to form ring.

Rnd 1: Ch 1, 14 sc in ring, join with sl st in first sc.

Rnd 2: *Ch 4, sl st in next sc; rep from * around, ending last rep with sl st in base of beg ch 4 - 14 loops. Place a marker on the last rnd to indicate right side and bottom end.

First Swirl: Ch 7, sl st between 2nd and 3rd loops.

Row 2: Ch 1, turn, work 14 sc in ch- 7 loop, sl st in next loop of Base - 14 sc.

Row 3: Ch 1, turn, dc in each sc, sl st in next loop of Base - 14 dc.

Row 4: Ch 1, turn, sc in each dc, sl st in same loop as Row 2.

Row 5: Turn,**ch 3, hdc in 3rd ch from hook* **- Picot made**, skip next sc, sc in next sc; rep from * across, sl st in same loop as Row 3, sl st in next loop of Base - 7 Picots.

2nd Swirl: Ch 7, turn, sl st between first 2 Picots.

Row 2: Ch 1, turn, work 14 sc in ch-7 loop, sl st in same loop of Base.

Row 3: Ch 1, turn, dc in each sc, sl st in next Picot.

Row 4: Ch 1, turn, sc in each dc across, sl st in next loop of Base.

Row 5: Turn,*Picot, skip next sc, sc in next sc; rep from * across, sl st in same Picot - 7 Picots.

3rd Swirl: Ch 7, turn, sl st between first 2 Picots.

Row 2: Ch 1, turn, work 14 sc in ch-7 loop, ch 1, sl st in next Picot.

Row 3: Ch 1, turn, dc in each sc, sl st in next Picot.

Row 4: Ch 1, turn, sc in each dc across, sl st in next Picot.

Row 5: Turn, *Picot, skip next sc, sc in next sc; rep from * across, sl st in same Picot - 7 Picots.

Repeat 3rd Swirl until panel measures 40.5" [103 cm] from beg, but Do Not Turn after last Swirl.

Ending Base: Ch 7, sl st in same Picot as join.

Row 1: Ch 1, turn, work 14 sc in ch-7 loop, sl st in next Picot of last Swirl.

Row 2: Turn, [Ch 4, skip next sc, sl st in next sc] 6 times, sl st in next Picot. Fasten off.

Weave in all ends.

To Complete: Lay panels out flat in the following color sequence: Pink, Green, White, Blue, Pink, Green, White, Blue.

Be sure to have markers all at one end of blanket.

Using matching colors, sew or crochet the panels together as desired.

Fringe: Cut remaining yarn into 10" [25.5 cm] lengths. Using 8 strands for each fringe, knot matching colors across both ends of blanket as desired.

Lullaby Baby Blanket

INTERMEDIATE

SHOPPING LIST

Yarn (DK/Sport Weight) LIGHT 3

[3.5 ounces, 295 yards (100 grams, 270 meters) per ball]:

- ☐ Main Color 4 balls

Crochet Hook

- ☐ Size 7 (4.50 mm) or size needed for gauge

SIZE INFORMATION

Size: 28" x 31" [71cm x 78.5 cm]

GAUGE INFORMATION

4 blocks of sts = 3" [7.5 cm] horizontally and vertically using **suggested** hook or any size hook which will give the correct stitch gauge or tension.

STITCH GUIDE

CL- Cluster; [Yarn over, draw up a loop in indicated st or sp, yo and draw through 2 loops on hook] 3 times, yo and pull through all 4 loops on hook.

Note: Blanket is worked in blocks of sts beg at the lower right corner and working diagonally to upper left corner.

INSTRUCTIONS

Row 1: Ch 5, CL in 5th ch from hook, ch 2, dc in same ch - 1st block made.

Mark this as right side.

Row 2: Ch 4, turn, CL in next ch-2 sp, ch 1, (sc, ch 3, CL, ch 2, dc) in turning (ch-sp) - 2 blocks made.

Row 3: Ch 4, turn, CL in next ch-2 sp, ch 1, (sc, ch 3, CL) in next ch-3 sp, ch 1, (sc, ch 3, CL, ch 2, dc) in turning (ch-sp) - 3 blocks made.

Row 4: Ch 4, turn, CL in first ch-2 sp, ch 1, *(sc, ch 3, CL) in next ch-3 sp, ch 1; rep from * to last ch-sp, (sc, ch 3, CL, ch 2, dc) in turning ch-sp.

Repeat Row 4 for pattern until 41 rows (41 blocks) have been completed, ending at lower left corner.

Row 42: Turn, sl st in next CL and next ch-3 sp,(ch 4, CL) in same sp, *(sc, ch 3, CL) in next ch-3 sp, ch 1; rep from * to last ch-sp, (sc, ch 3, CL, ch 2, dc) in turning ch-sp.

Row 43: Ch 4, turn, CL in next ch-2 sp, ch 1, *(sc, ch 3, CL) in next ch-3 sp, ch 1; rep from * to last ch-sp, sl st in turning ch.

Rows 44-51: Rep Rows 42 and 43 four times.

Row 52: Turn, sl st in next CL and ch-3 sp, (ch 4, CL) in same sp, *(sc, ch 3, CL) in next ch-3 sp, ch 1; rep from * to last ch-sp, sl st in turning ch-sp.

Repeat Row 52 until only one block remains in last row. Do not fasten off.

Edging:

Rnd 1: Ch 1, turn, sc in next CL, 3 sc in corner, *sc evenly along edge of blanket, working 2 or 3 sc in each ch loop (making sure edge lays flat), work 3 sc in corner; rep from * around, join with sl st in first sc.

Rnd 2: *Ch 4, skip next sc, sc in next sc; rep from * around, adjusting sts as needed at corner to work sc in center sc of 3-sc in each corner, join with sl st in base of beg ch-4. Fasten off.

Weave in all ends.

Playful Colors Blanket

INTERMEDIATE

SHOPPING LIST

Yarn (Worsted Weight) MEDIUM 4
[1.75 ounces, 109 yards
(50 grams, 100 meters) per ball]:

- ☐ Main Color-Variegated 9 balls
- ☐ Contrast Color-White 5 balls

Crochet Hook

- ☐ Size J-10 (6.00 mm)
  or size needed for gauge

SIZE INFORMATION

Size: 28.5" x 45" [72 cm x 114 cm]

GAUGE INFORMATION

4 pattern repeats (1 sc, 2 dc) to 3.5" [9 cm] and 8 rows to 3.25" [8 cm] measured over pattern using **suggested** hook or any size hook which will give the correct stitch gauge or tension.

Note: This blanket is worked lengthwise from side to side.

INSTRUCTIONS

To Make: Using MC, ch 146.

Base Row: (Sc, 2dc) in 2nd ch from hook, *skip next 2 ch, (sc, 2 dc) in next ch; rep from * to last 3 ch, skip next 2 ch, sc in last ch.

Row 1: Ch 1 (counts as first sc), 2 dc in first sc, *skip 2 dc, (sc, 2 dc) in next sc; rep from * to last 3 sts, skip 2 dc, sc in top of turning ch.

Rows 2-5: Work as Row 1.

Rows 6 and 7: Using CC, work as Row 1.

Rows 8-13: Using MC, work as Row 1.

Repeat Rows 6-13 eight times more. Fasten off.

Border: With right side facing, join CC in top right corner and work as follows:

Rnd 1: Ch 1 (counts as first sc), *sc evenly along side to corner, (sc, ch 2, sc) in corner; rep from * twice more, sc evenly to last corner, (sc, ch 2) in first corner, join with sl st in first sc.

Rnds 2 and 3: Work as Rnd 1.

Rnd 4: *Ch 3, skip next sc, sl st in next sc (or ch-2 sp at corner when you come to it); rep from * around entire outside edge of blanket, join with sl st in top of beg ch-3. Fasten off.

General Instructions

ABBREVIATIONS

"	inches
beg	begin or beginning
CC	Contrast Color
ch	chain
cm	centimeters
dc	double crochet
dec	decrease or decreasing
gm	gram
hdc	half double crochet
inc	increase or increasing
MC	Main Color
mm	millimeter
rem	remain or remaining
rep	repeat
rnd(s)	round(s)
sc	single crochet
sl	slip
sp(s)	spaces(s)
st(s)	stitch(es)
tog	together
tr	treble crochet
yo	yarn over hook

*** or **** work instructions following or between * or ** as many more times as indicated in addition to the first time.

() or [ ] work enclosed instructions as many times as specified by the number immediately following or work all enclosed instructions in the stitch or space indicated or contains explanatory remarks

— the number(s) given at the end of a row or round denote(s) the number of stitches or spaces you should have on that row or round.

BEGINNER	Projects for first-time crocheters using basic stitches. Minimal shaping.
EASY	Projects using yarn with basic stitches, repetitive stitch patterns, simple color changes, and simple shaping and finishing.
INTERMEDIATE	Projects using a variety of techniques, such as basic lace patterns or color patterns, mid-level shaping and finishing.
EXPERIENCED	Projects with intricate stitch patterns, techniques and dimension, such as non-repeating patterns, multi-color techniques, fine threads, small hooks, detailed shaping and refined finishing.

Yarn Weight Symbol & Names	LACE 0	SUPER FINE 1	FINE 2	LIGHT 3	MEDIUM 4	BULKY 5	SUPER BULKY 6	JUMBO 7
Type of Yarns in Category	Fingering, size 10 crochet thread	Sock, Fingering, Baby	Sport, Baby	DK, Light Worsted	Worsted, Afghan, Aran	Chunky, Craft, Rug	Super Bulky, Roving	Jumbo, Roving
Crochet Gauge* Ranges in Single Crochet to 4" (10 cm)	32-42 sts**	21-32 sts	16-20 sts	12-17 sts	11-14 sts	8-11 sts	6-9 sts	5 sts and fewer
Advised Hook Size Range	Steel*** 6 to 8, Regular hook B-1	B-1 to E-4	E-4 to 7	7 to I-9	I-9 to K-10½	K-10½ to M/N-13	M/N-13 to Q	Q and larger

*GUIDELINES ONLY: The chart above reflects the most commonly used gauges and hook sizes for specific yarn categories.

CROCHET TERMINOLOGY		
UNITED STATES		INTERNATIONAL
slip stitch (slip st)	=	single crochet (sc)
single crochet (sc)	=	double crochet (dc)
half double crochet (hdc)	=	half treble crochet (htr)
double crochet (dc)	=	treble crochet (tr)
treble crochet (tr)	=	double treble crochet (dtr)
double treble crochet (dtr)	=	triple treble crochet (ttr)
triple treble crochet (ttr)	=	quadruple treble crochet (qtr)
skip	=	miss

CROCHET HOOKS

U.S.	B-1	C-2	D-3	E-4	F-5	G-6	7	H-8	I-9	J-10	K-10½	L-11	M/N-13	N/P-15	P/Q	Q	S
Metric - mm	2.25	2.75	3.25	3.5	3.75	4	4.5	5	5.5	6	6.5	8	9	10	15	16	19

Slip Knot

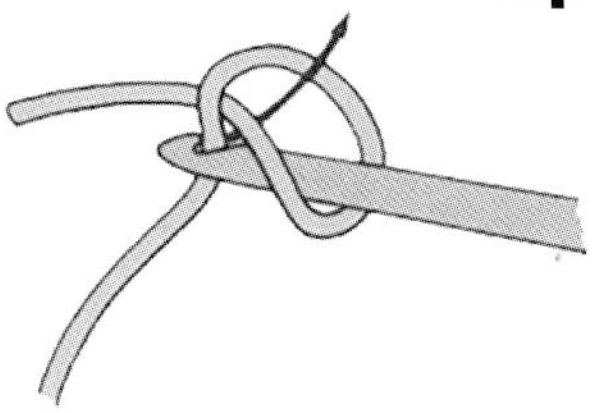

1. Make a loop, then hook another loop through it.

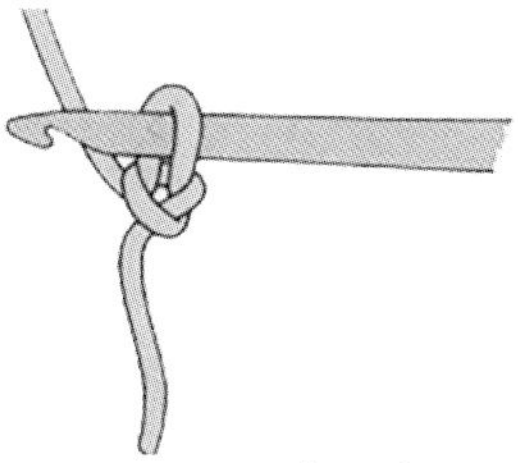

2. Tighten gently and slide the knot up to the hook.

Chain Stitch (ch)

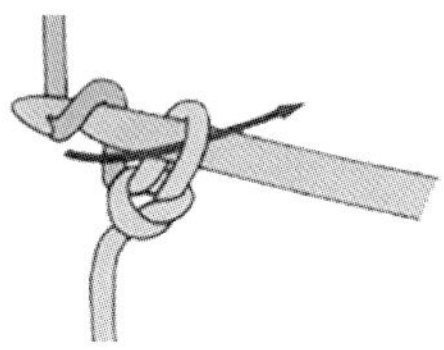

1. Yarn over hook (yo) and draw the yarn through to form a new loop without tightening up the previous one.

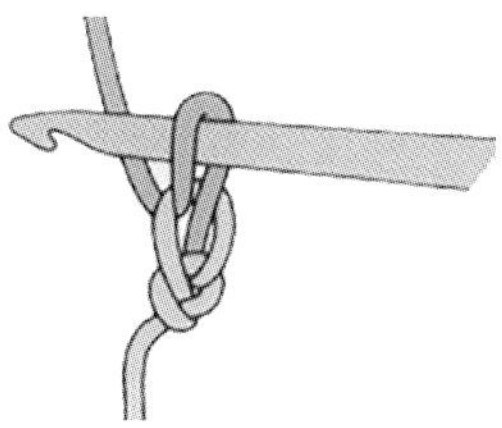

2. Repeat to form as many chains (ch) as required. Do not count the slip knot as a stitch.

Slip Stitch (sl st)

This is the shortest crochet stitch and unlike other stitches is not used on its own to produce a fabric. It is used for joining, shaping and where necessary carrying the yarn to another part of the fabric for the next stage.

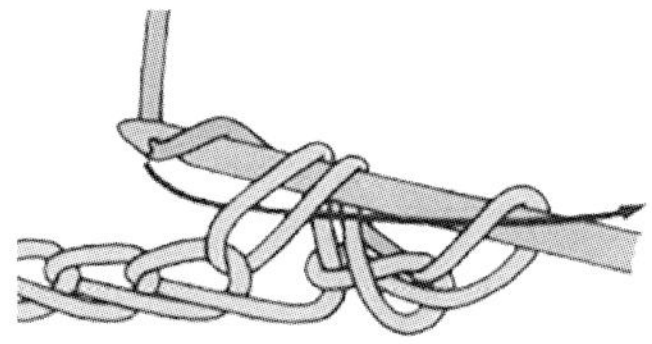

Insert hook into work (second chain from hook), yarn over hook (yo) and draw the yarn through both the work and loop on hook in one movement.

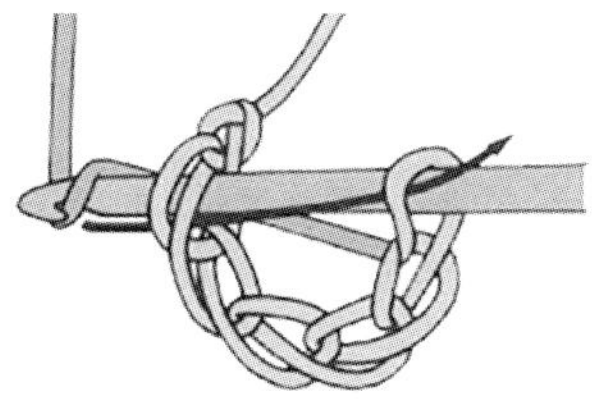

To join a chain ring with a slip stitch (sl st), insert hook into first chain (ch), yarn over hook (yo) and draw through both the work and the yarn on hook in one movement.

Single Crochet (sc)

1. Insert the hook into the work (2nd chain (ch) from hook on starting chain), *yarn over hook (yo) and draw yarn through the work only.

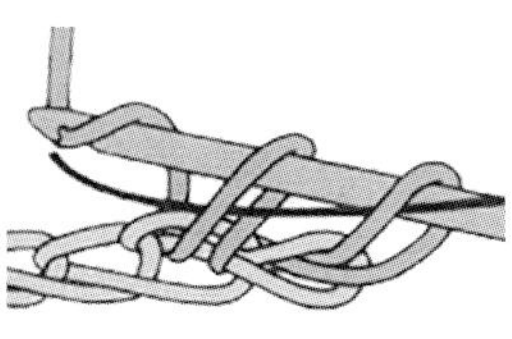

2. Yarn over hook (yo) again and draw the yarn through both loops on the hook.

3. 1 single crochet (sc) made. Insert hook into next stitch: repeat (rep) from * in step 1.

Half Double Crochet (hdc)

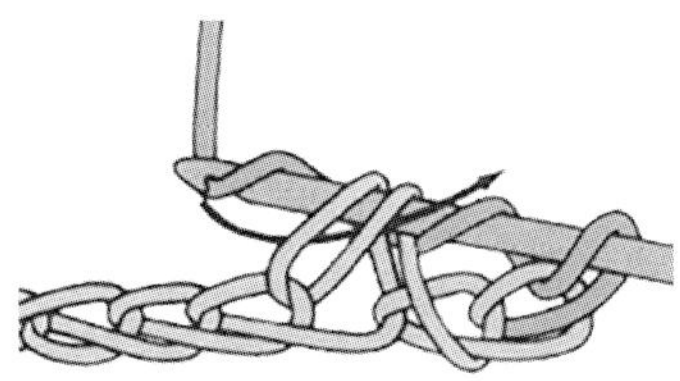

1. Yarn over hook (yo) and insert the hook into the work (3rd chain (ch) from hook on starting chain) and draw through the work only.

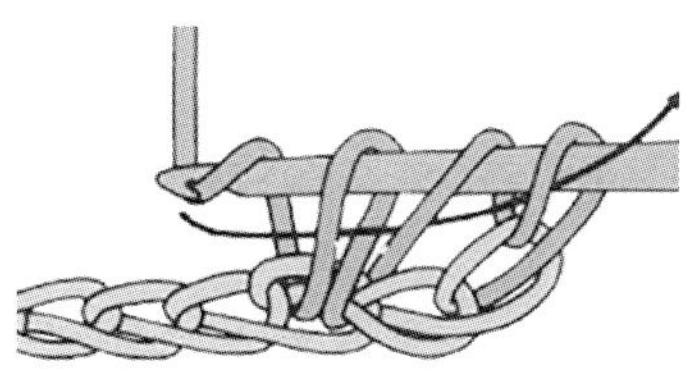

2. Yarn over hook (yo) again and draw through all three loops on the hook.

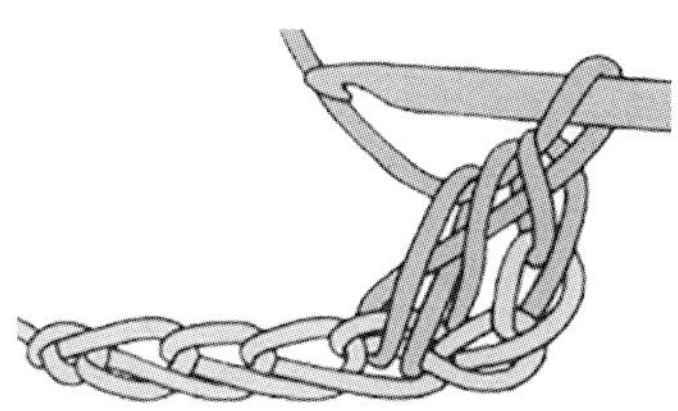

3. 1 hdc made. Yarn over hook (yo), insert hook into next stitch (st), repeat (rep) from step 2.

Double Crochet (dc)

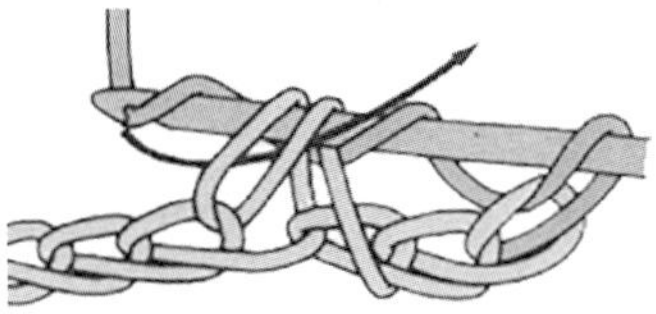

1. Yarn over hook (yo) and insert the hook into the work (4th chain from hook on starting chain) yo and draw through the work only.

2. Yarn over hook (yo) and draw through the first two loops only.

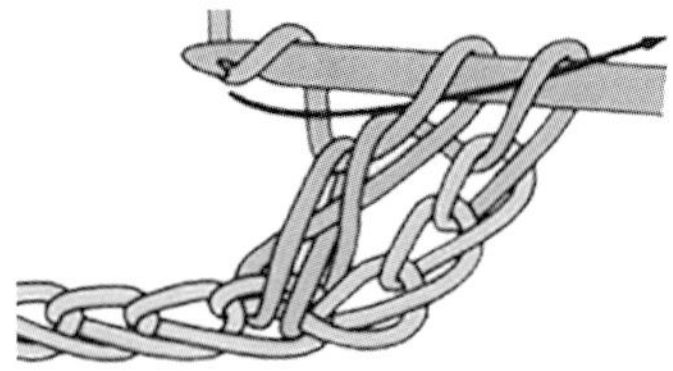

3. Yarn over hook (yo) and draw through the last two loops on the hook.

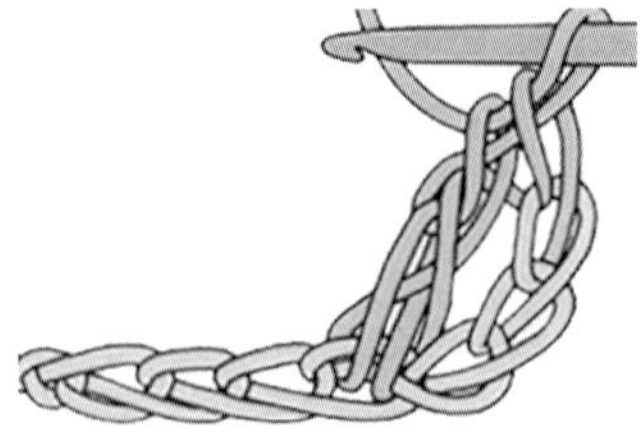

4. 1 dc made. Yarn over hook (yo), insert hook into next stitch (st); yo and draw through work only, repeat (rep) from step 2.

Treble Crochet (tr)

Work same as given for Double Crochet (dc) above,
but in Step 1 yarn over hook (yo) twice, then rep Step 2 twice.

Yarn Information

Projects in this book were made with fingering, sport and worsted weight yarns. Any brand of yarn may be used. It is best to refer to yardage/meters when determining how many balls or skeins to purchase. Remember, to arrive at the finished size, it is the GAUGE/TENSION that is important, not the brand of yarn. For your convenience, listed below are the specific yarn ranges used to create our photographed models.

Sweet Ribbons Blanket
Mary Maxim Starlette
Bernat Satin

Scalloped Border Blanket
Mary Maxim Baby's Best

Butterfly Afghan
Mary Maxim Baby's Best

Choo-Choo Blankie
Mary Maxim Twinkle

Baby Swirls Blanket
Mary Maxim Baby's Best

Lullaby Baby Blanket
Mary Maxim Sugar Baby Stripes

Playful Colors Blanket
Mary Maxim Baby Kashmere

Made In China